G000255413

Contents

Yes wherl is
the foto

Introduction

Welcome to Living Life to the Full.

I'm Professor Chris Williams, Emeritus Professor of Psychosocial Psychiatry at the University of Glasgow. I've been working for the last 15 years looking at ways of helping people improve their lives. We can all sometimes feel down or fed up, stressed or worried, or that we aren't good enough. However, there are things you can do to make positive changes in each of these areas. It also involves rediscovering the things you already do that are good for you- and how to build these in your life.

I'm an expert in the talking treatment called cognitive behaviour therapy- or CBT. This is often offered to help people with low mood or stress. It can help prevent problems such as these developing in the first place. Because of this it is increasingly being introduced into schools and other settings where young people go to help you learn key skills that can give you a growing sense of control over how you feel and how you react. These are skills that can last a lifetime.

The course is a series of chapters and linked course modules that can also be taught in classroom settings. The same resources including additional videos and reading materials are available under license at www.llttfyp.com.

I welcome feedback, suggestions and comments. I firmly believe that skills such as these can make a real difference to your and my life. There's no quick fixes, and to really get good at using some of the skills that are taught will take practice, - but who doesn't need to learn how to be calmer, more confident and in control, happier and someone others turn to for answers?

Discover more at: www.llttfyp.com

Linked course for primary schools: www.WeEatElephants.com

Information for educators and practitioners: www.fiveareas.com

If you need more help: Reach out and tell someone- a teacher, your doctor, a trusted family member or friend. Get the help you need. Don't suffer in silence.

Young person version co-ordinated by the Canadian Mental Health Association, supported by grants from Bell and RBC Children's mental health project.

Introduction to Chapter 1

All of us from time to time feel happy - glad, even joyful.
When we feel like this it's a great feeling isn't it?

But sometimes we feel bad. Down, low, sad, stressed,
anxious, worried, panicky, angry or embarrassed.

Did you know we feel like we do for a reason? That's
what this chapter is about. It provides you with the keys to
understanding you and how you feel.

Have you ever had a bad cold? You notice the runny nose
and sore throat, the itchy eyes and the aches, pains and
coughs. How we feel in our bodies also affects how we
feel emotionally, what we think, and how we react and
relate to others. So, when we have that cold, we might
feel emotionally numbed, and not able to enjoy things
as before. It might feel harder to think things through,
give a talk in class, or make important decisions. If we
were feeling ill like that, we might find we choose to wear
different clothes at home, or eat or drink different foods. We
also might relate to others differently - making sure that our
illness is clearly communicated to them.

This illustrates an important point. That how we feel is
affected by our bodies, thoughts, and actions as well as
what goes on around us.

This chapter will help you discover what makes you tick –
and how you can gain a sense of control over how you feel
and how you act. You can't change what you don't know–
and by the end of this chapter you'll know a lot more about
what makes you feel good – or bad.

Chapter 1

UNDERSTANDING
YOUR FEELINGS

Friends hate me
Someone close is really sick
LOST MY JOB
FAILED TEST OR EXAM
We broke up
Being bullied
BEING ILL
NO ONE TO TALK TO
Got criticised
Best friend ignored me
Bad day at school/work
I'm all alone
GOT KICKED OFF THE TEAM
I've got no money
Too much to do

You feel bad because you're in a vicious cycle

The way you feel is affected by things that happen to you. Like the bad things on the opposite page. Those things are all outside of you. Sometimes, you can change what's happening outside, but often, you can't do much about them.

And when you allow them to affect your mood, the vicious cycle kicks in and you feel worse and worse and worse ...

Turn over to see how it works

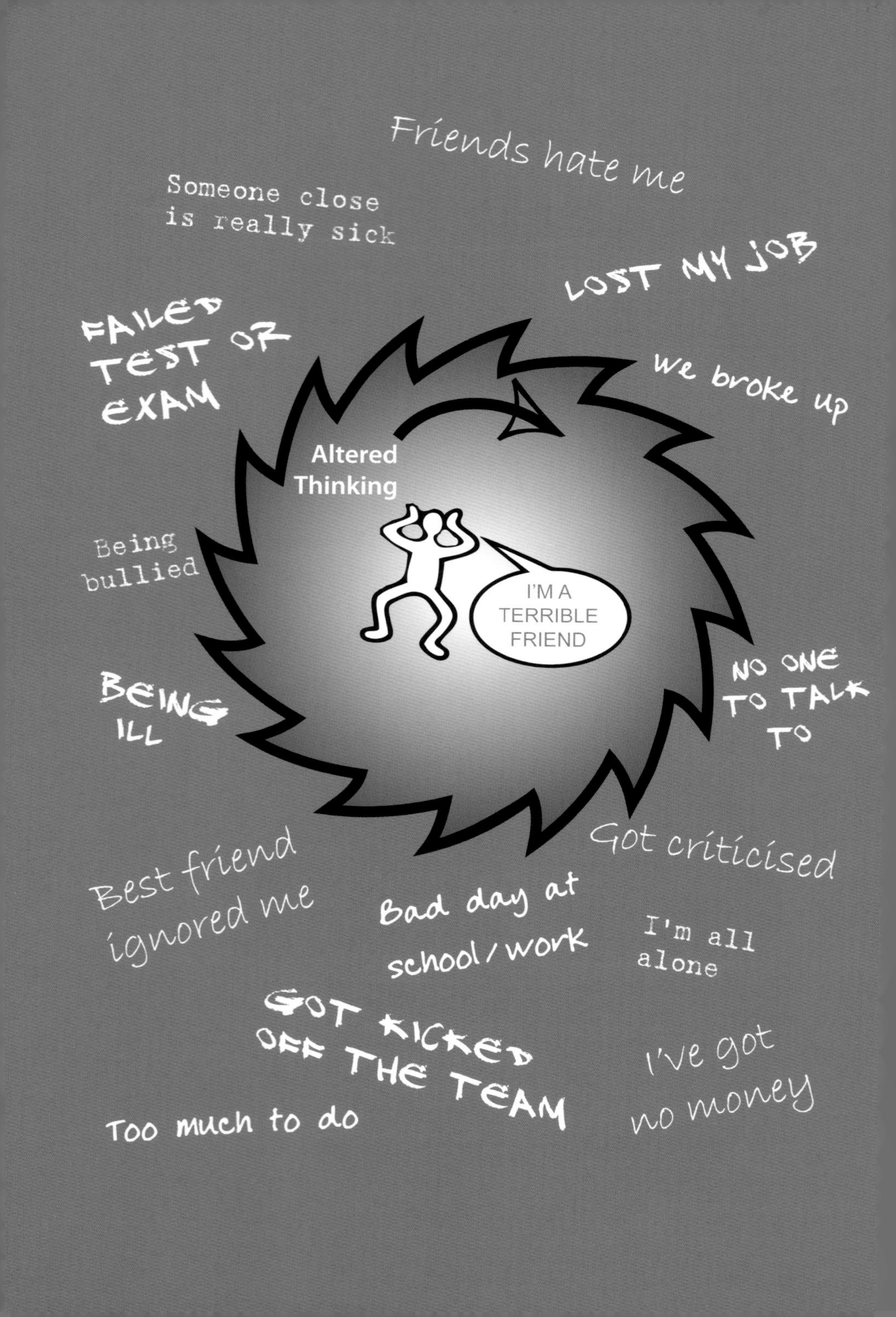

1. First, an outside event affects you

When something happens, you naturally notice it and think about it.

Example: You forget your friend's birthday

You may think "I'm a terrible friend!"

This is called Altered Thinking

Altered thinking can set off a chain reaction inside you that affects the way you feel and what you do.

When your altered thinking is negative (like "I'm useless"), the vicious cycle is triggered and you can end up really low, not getting out of bed and even feeling sick.

Let's watch the vicious cycle in action

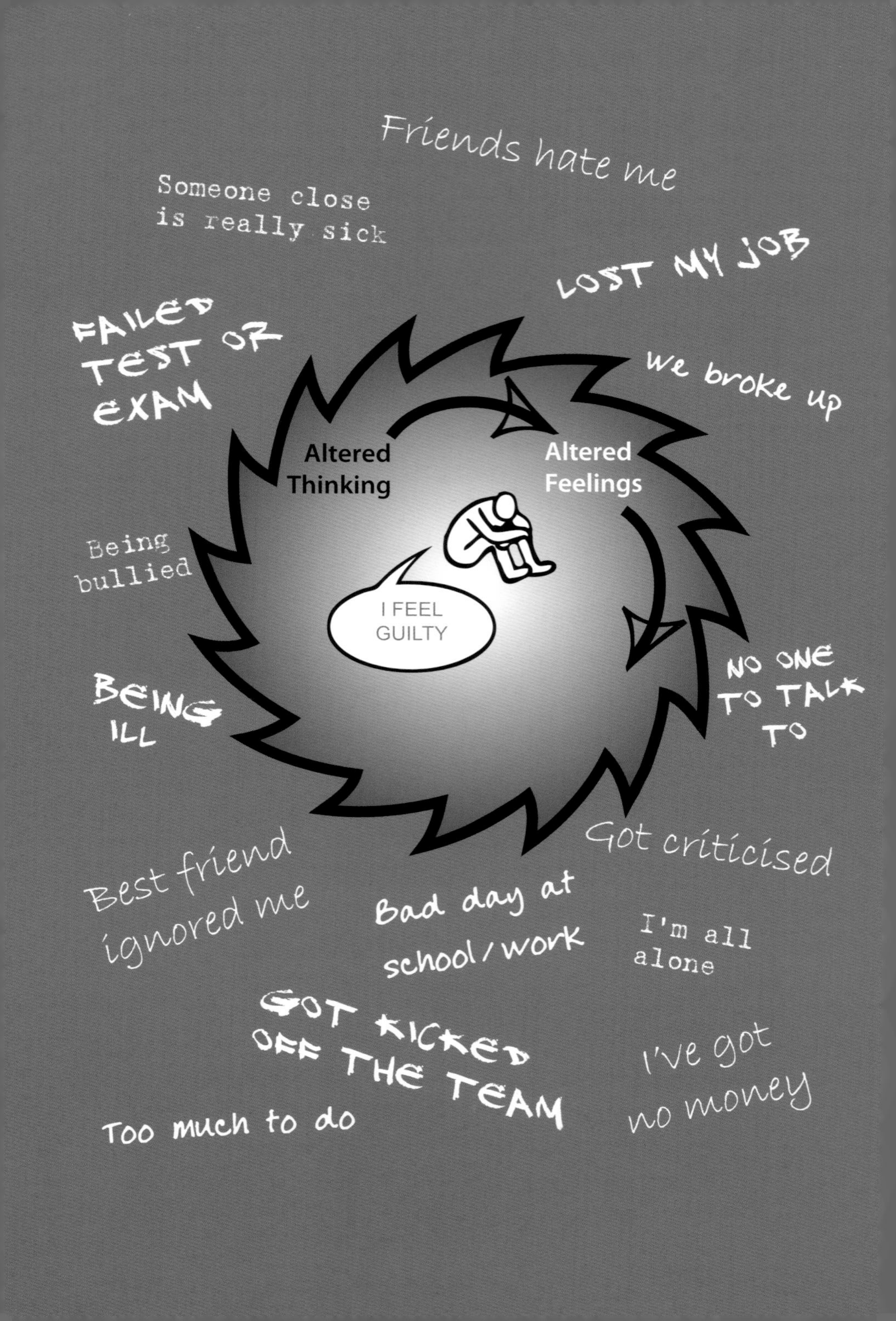
Friends hate me
Someone close is really sick
LOST MY JOB
FAILED TEST OR EXAM
We broke up
Altered Thinking
Altered Feelings
Being bullied
I FEEL GUILTY
NO ONE TO TALK TO
BEING ILL
Got criticised
Best friend ignored me
Bad day at school / work
I'm all alone
GOT KICKED OFF THE TEAM
I've got no money
Too much to do

2. Altered thinking leads to...
3. altered feelings

If you think "I'm a terrible friend!" you're going to feel pretty low, sad or guilty.

Maybe you feel as if you've let your friend down, or you might feel guilty because you know you should have been more organised.

So now what happens?

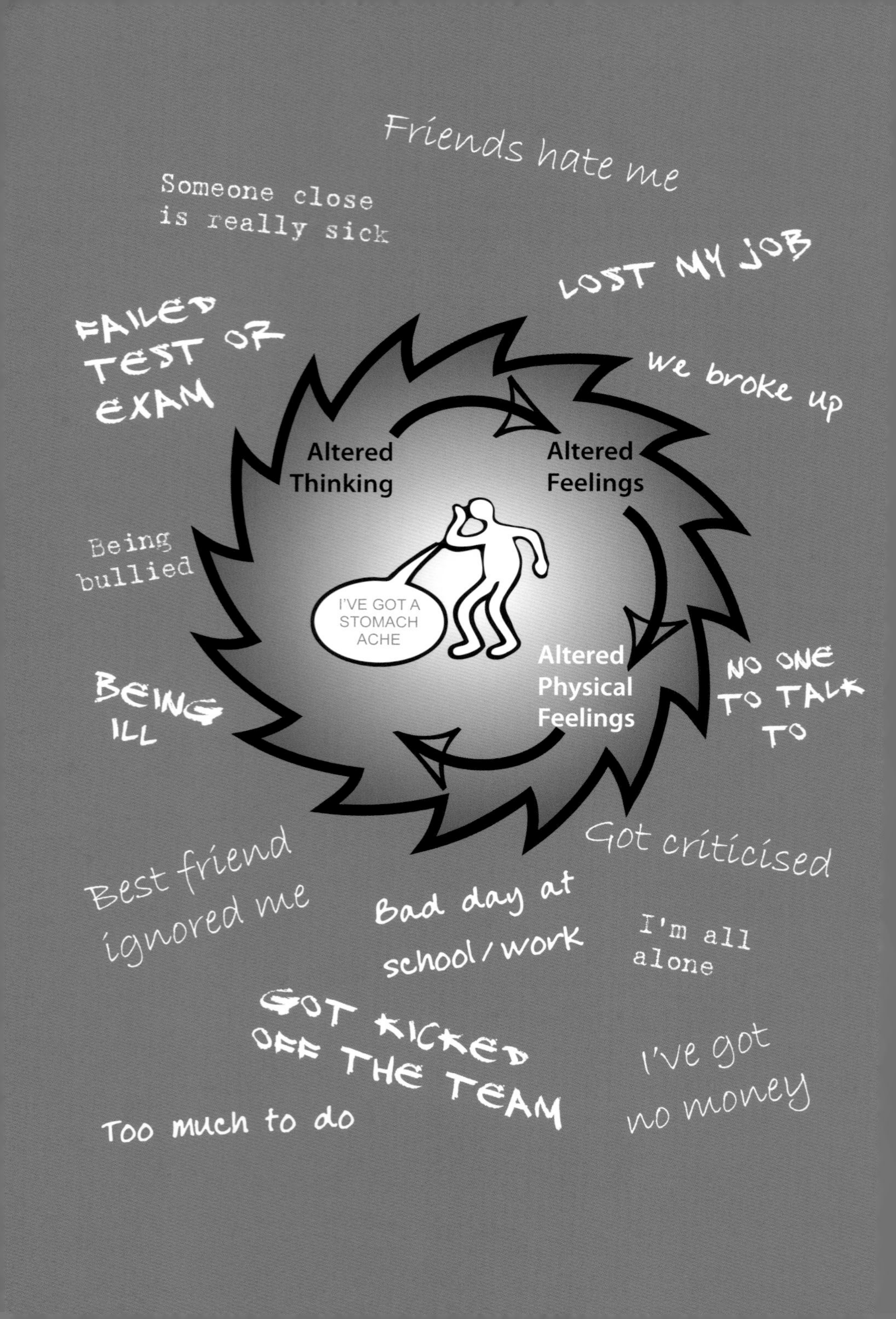

4. Altered feelings lead to altered physical symptoms

When you feel low or guilty, you can get sweaty and tense and your stomach or your head can ache. Sometimes you can feel really tired.

Your hands might feel clammy, or you feel really tense and can't sit still.

Ever had a sinking feeling or felt your heart racing? It's probably that old vicious cycle spinning round!

What next?

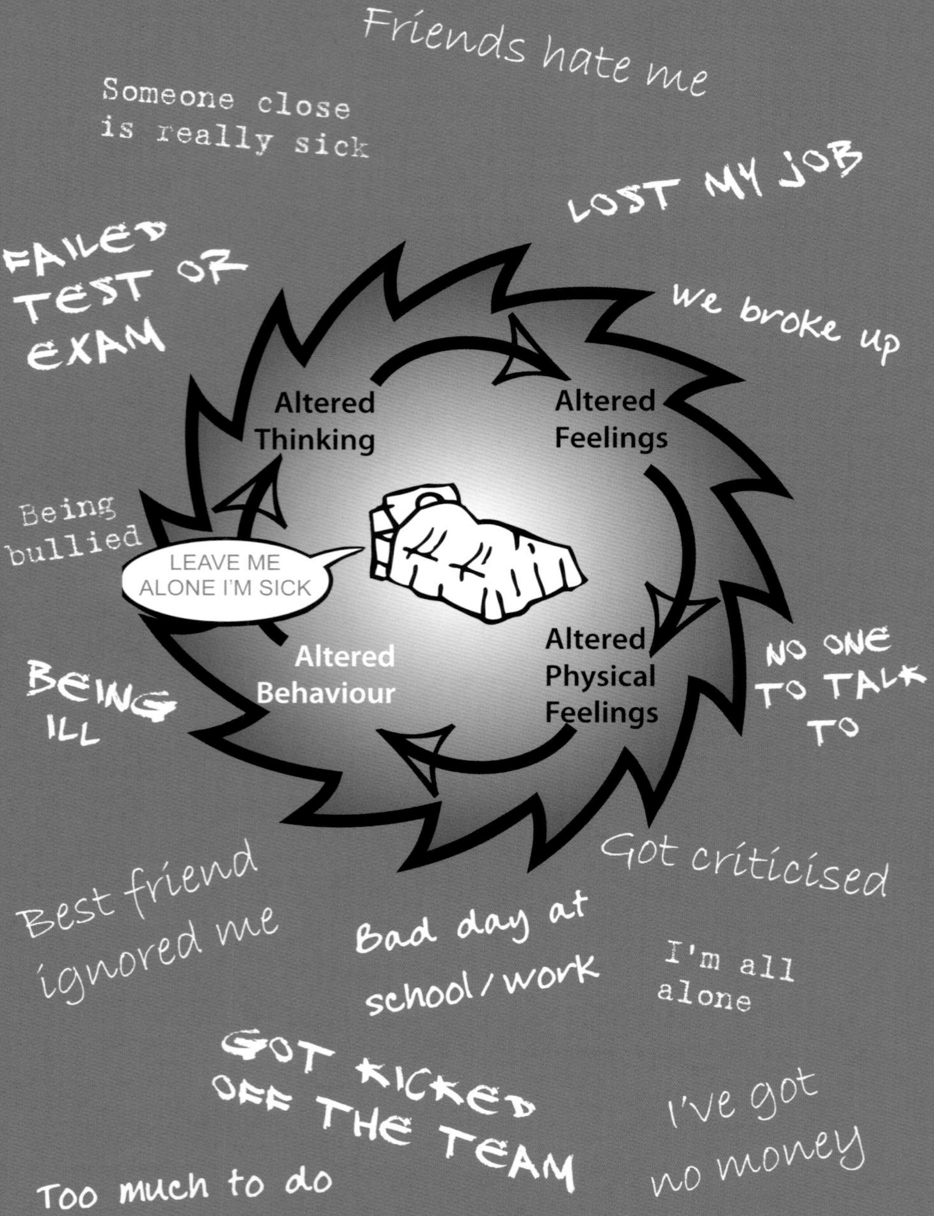

5. Altered physical symptoms lead to altered behaviour

It's only natural. You're really tired, you have a headache or maybe feel tense, so you don't feel like going out, or even getting up. You steer clear of people who might ask if you sent a card or present. You stay in and hardly do any exercise. You're not eating right and you seem to catch all the bugs that are going around.

You even end up at the doctor's, asking why you can't seem to shake off this virus you've had for weeks.

And you know what happens then? The cycle goes round again, only this time, you're already sick, staying in bed and fed up, so you get even worse.

Vicious, these vicious cycles, aren't they?

Now it's time to think about how the five areas apply to you.

Now what about you?

COMPLETE YOUR OWN FIVE AREAS ASSESSMENT

You've read about how you might react if you missed your friends birthday. Do you fall into other vicious cycles from time to time?

Here's how to play detective and work out how the vicious cycle affects you.

Choose two recent times when you felt bad. To start with, don't pick times that are really upsetting or distressing. Instead choose situations when you felt a bit down, fed up, angry, stressed, scared, frustrated, guilty, ashamed, tired, or in pain.

Now use the next two pages to work out how you reacted.

Pen at the ready?

Now's time to spot that vicious cycle!

People and Events

Altered Thinking

People and Events

Altered Behaviour

People and Events

Altered Feelings

Altered Physical Feelings

People and Events

YOUR VICIOUS CYCLE

Did you fall into a vicious cycle?

If you felt bad, it's likely the vicious cycle was spinning. What were the outside events like people/difficult situations? Did what you think affect how you felt - in your feelings and physical feelings? How did this affect what you did?

Did anything look familiar? Patterns of thinking, feeling or body reactions often repeat again and again. Did the cycle start to spin and make you feel even worse?

Stopping your cycle spinning takes practise. If you're feeling worse than usual it can feel hard to break the cycle.

Now for the *good* news!

YOU CAN STOP THE CYCLE!

You know the great thing about cycles? They turn both ways!

In the same way that just one thing (an altered thought) led to everything else getting worse, you can start to make it better by changing one thing.

Just by eating differently or doing more exercise, or changing the way you think about some things, you can affect **all the other things in the cycle** and start to feel better.

Sounds too easy? Turn over for an example.

How to stop the cycle

1. You're walking down the corridor at school and someone you know ignores you

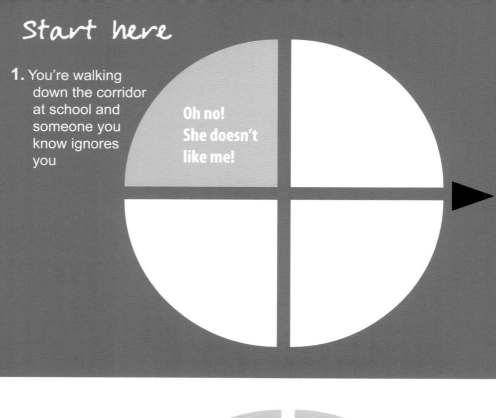

Oh no! She doesn't like me!

4. You have no energy and maybe can't sleep that night worrying about what happened - altered physical symptoms

Oh no! She doesn't like me!

I feel down

What's wrong with me? I feel tired and exhausted.

I don't want to see anyone at the moment

Now let's stop the cycle!

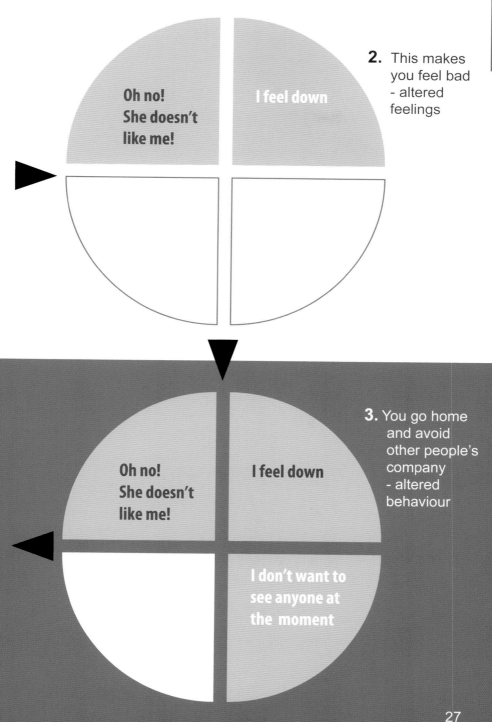

2. This makes you feel bad - altered feelings

Oh no! She doesn't like me!

I feel down

3. You go home and avoid other people's company - altered behaviour

Oh no! She doesn't like me!

I feel down

I don't want to see anyone at the moment

27

1. You're walking down the corridor at school and someone you know ignores you

Poor Sarah, she must be upset, I wonder what's wrong?

4. You arrange to see Sarah later and discuss practical things you can do to help

Poor Sarah, she must be upset, I wonder what's wrong?

Is there anything I can do?

I feel really great, alert and strong.

I feel good about myself because I'm helping someone else.

See how it works?

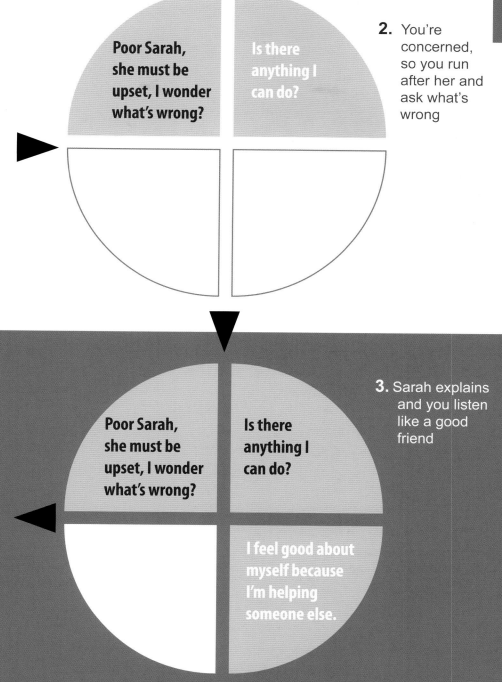

2. You're concerned, so you run after her and ask what's wrong

3. Sarah explains and you listen like a good friend

YOU
HAVE
CONTROL

You just need to change one thing

You can take control and stop the vicious cycle by changing just one thing - your thinking, your diet, your activities - almost anything. And it doesn't have to be a big thing!

You could start by changing the way you eat. By going out just one time. By changing the way you think about things.

If you manage to do something about just one thing, you'll break the vicious cycle, stop it spinning down and down and start to feel better straight away.

Go make a plan!

Don't just sit there, make a plan! Planner sheet

1. What am I going to do?

2. When am I going to do it?

3. What problems or difficulties could arise, and how can I overcome them?

Is my planned task -

	Yes	No
Q. Useful for improving my well-being?	☐	☐
Q. Specific, so that I will know when I have done it?	☐	☐
Q. Realistic, practical and achievable?	☐	☐

OK, how did it go?

Review Sheet

What did you plan to do? Write it here:

If yes:

1. What went well?

2. What didn't go so well?

3. What have you learned from what happened?

4. How are you going to apply what you have learned?

Did you try to do it?

Yes

No

If no: what stopped you?

Internal things (forgot, not enough time, put it off, didn't think I could do it, couldn't see the point etc.).

External things (other people, work or home issues etc.).

How could you have planned to tackle these things?

NEXT STEPS...

Use the five areas vicious cycle to make sense of why you feel the way you do. Remember, that's not all you've discovered. You've also learned some targets for change that will make a big difference.

What changes do you need to make in each of the five areas? When you've sorted your current problem, you might want to work on something else in your life.

You can get added help and support by working through the free linked online courses at www.llttfyp.com.

Go for it!

Introduction to Chapter 2

Do you ever wake up in the morning and think - "I just can't be bothered doing anything!" You feel tried and not really wanting to do much at all. That feeling goes away when we get a few good night's sleep or when we slowly come around as the day continues. But what if that feeling sticks around far longer?

Have you ever noticed that if you want some help with something, sometimes someone who is busy responds a lot faster than someone who has little on? That busy person somehow seems to have more energy and focus- and can get things done. In contrast, the person who has less on their plate might put things off and say they'll help later. There's an important truth here - that the less we do, the less likely we are to do anything.

That's important because if we hit a rough patch and start to feel stressed, hassled or down, it can be so easy to feel overwhelmed and start to do less and less. We can withdraw from others, or take to our beds for longer. And a cycle can be set up where the less we do, the worse we feel, and the worse we feel, the less we do.

That's what this chapter focuses on. It will help you discover how you can improve how you feel by choosing to change what you do. It identifies the ingredients for feeling good – having a daily routine that balances the *should* stuff and the *good* stuff. It helps you identify those good activities- the things you can do that will make you feel better.

Don't forget, you're in control.

DO
THI
THAT MAKE
YOU FEEL
BETTER

I feel too sick to do things

I feel tired all the time

ys

I hardly see anyone outside of school these days

Sometimes I'm scared to go out

I haven't even got the energy to read this book

I do what I have to do, and no more

I can hardly be bothered getting dressed in the morning

Know what? You're in a vicious cycle.

When you feel low, you tend to stop doing things. You don't go out so much and you avoid seeing friends. As a result, you feel even lower, and then you feel like doing even less.

It's like: the less you do, the worse you feel, the worse you feel, the less you do. And it keeps going round and round and round ...

Things can get quite vicious

So, what's going on?

1

Symptoms make things hard.
Low, not sleeping/tired.
Scared, fed up.
Can't be bothered.

4

Count the cost.
Feel worse, lose confidence.
Less pleasure, less achievement,
see friends less.
You feel worse and worse.

2

Struggle to do things.
Everything seems harder/more effort.
Things seem pointless/not enjoyed.
Going through the motions.

3

**Cut down/avoid things
that seem too hard.**
Do less and less.
Only do things you must/
should do.
"You" time squeezed out.

Turn over to break the cycle

WOW!

Do you know what you just did?

You broke the cycle!

All it took was a little bit of positive action - turning that page.

Now all you have to do is take another tiny step, then another and another.

What steps? That's what this chapter is about - to show you the easy steps you can take to break that cycle into bits and start feeling better.

It involves making choices. Choosing to do things that make you feel better, rather than hiding away feeling worse and worse.

So here's what you do next

Think about yesterday

Start by thinking about the last 24 hours. Write down everything you have done. Include things like talking to a friend on the phone, going to the gym, watching TV, etc. Then score them out of ten for pleasure, achievement and feeling close to other people. The first few spaces are filled in to show you how to do it.

Doing this will help you understand what's good in your life and also to realise what's missing.

About closeness

Feeling close to others is really important, but when we're down, we sometimes hide away. If your diary doesn't have enough things with a good closeness score, this chapter will help you sort that out.

	Pleasure	Achievement	Closeness
Talking to Alison on the phone	9	3	10
Cleaning my room	1	10	0

Activity	Pleasure	Achievement	Closeness
~~Asking~~ Eat	10	10	0
Sleep	10	0	0
~~ Exercise	5	10	10
Spoke with people	5	0	10
played Guitar	10	10	0
Walked with dog	9	10	10
Took the bins out for m...	0	10	0
went to pro musician w/ friend	5	10	10
Study for a test instrum	0	10	0
	50	70	40

ANYTHING MISSING FROM YOUR DIARY?

Are you ignoring important things?

Eating well, looking after yourself, keeping up with homework, blogging, talking to friends, eating with family or friends, and doing hobbies - they can all seem too much trouble when you're down.

The problem is, avoiding these essentials makes you feel worse and can get you in a mess. So here's what to do: choose one thing that wasn't in your diary but should have been, and do it - now.

Make that call. Do some tidying up. Get out of your room and reconnect with people. You'll feel loads better afterwards and you'll be able to add it to your diary and put a 10 in the 'achievement' box!

FIND SOMETHING TO GET UP FOR

Rebuild your routine

Having to get out of bed to walk the dog or to go running can be a real pain, especially on cold mornings, but it's also a great way to feel better.

No dog? Don't run? Then make yourself a routine with other things. Getting up and showering. Eating breakfast. Playing your music. Getting on the bus. Making the most of the activities you can do.

And if you rebuild your routine with things that involve others (phone a friend every morning, study at a friend's house after school), you'll feel even better because of that closeness thing we mentioned before.

It needs to be a daily routine, too. Choose something every single day that you need to get up and out of bed for. Don't sleep all day on the weekends - remember, the less you do the worse you feel, the worse you feel, the less you do.

Now make a list of the things you enjoy

Check your diary and pick out the things you did that scored highly for pleasure, achievement or closeness to others. Write them down here.

_____

_____

_____

_____

_____

_____

_____

_____

_____

_____

These are things that make you feel good. Planning to do more activities like this can help.

But also, is there anything missing from your day?

What about things you've stopped doing?

Your diary may not contain all the things you like to do, so have a look through this list and tick the ones that apply to you - stuff you used to enjoy but haven't felt like doing lately.

What are the things you value and see as important for you to do?

Watching sports ☐

Going out with friends ☐

Listening to music ☐

Watching a movie ☐

Playing a sport ☐

Phoning friends ☐

Playing with pets ☐

Going to concerts or gigs ☐

Going for a walk ☐

Exercising ☐

Going to after school activities ☐

Playing a musical instrument ☐

Reading a good book ☑

Doing drama ☐

Going to church, temple, mosque, or synagogue ☐

Helping other people ☐

Well ticked!

Now we're going to make a plan

Aim for the following

You know what makes you feel good.

Across each day and week you need to get a mix of activities that help.

Start with the activities you can change most easily.

Aim for variety so you address each of the key areas:

1. Pleasure - things that make you feel good.

2. Achievement: things you value and see as important.

3. Closeness: where you connect with important others.

4. Finally don't forget to do things that are important and necessary.

Each of these activities breaks the vicious cycle and makes you feel better.

But don't rush. Some activities need to be built up to slowly.

_____'S
PLAN

(Write your name in the blank)

One of the reasons we feel worse when we stop doing things, is the fact that it's usually the things we like that we avoid first.

No wonder life seems to go down and down!

To start it going up again, you need to pick good things to fill your day with. Not all the time - just one thing to start with. So, once you've got a bit of a routine going, the next step of your plan is to look at the lists you just made and pick one of the things on them.

Pick something that used to give you pleasure or a sense of achievement. Or something that you think is worthwhile or made you feel close to others.

Just one.

Now write it here in big letters

_____

_____

_____

Good

You've just written down the thing you're going to start doing again.

It's all about planning steps that take you forwards.

But some activities may be good for you, but seem just too hard to do all at once. You need to work up to doing them step by step.

How?

Have a look at the example opposite.

For example:

Connor used to like meeting his friends for a coffee, but since he's been fed up, he hasn't had the energy for it. This is what he wrote in his plan for getting back to meeting them.

1. Practice getting to the coffee shop I like.

2. Have a coffee by myself. Enjoy the taste and smell of the coffee and being with others in the shop.

3. Phone, text or email a friend and ask if they can meet me for a coffee.

4. Meet up with them - and have a good time.

5. Decide to do it again - and ask a couple more people.

6. Arrange to meet some new people as well - so I'm widening the group I meet.

7. Have fun when I meet and feel the difference!

Connor knew he could take one step a day, or one step a week, it didn't matter. What mattered was having a plan and making steady progress towards getting some fun back in his life.

Right, that's enough of Connor. Now back to your plan.

Write down an activity that you need to build up to step by step here

_____

_____

_____

Now think about the little steps you can take towards doing it again. Make them really small and un-scary. Don't be ambitious, be easy on yourself. And don't worry if you have to keep crossing things out, there's plenty of space.

1. I'm going to ~~~~ make time
2. Then I'm going to ~~~~ go ~~~~ walking
3. Next, I'm going to ~~~~ do homework
4. Then I'm going to ~~~~ Eat
5. ~~~~
6. ~~~~
7.
8.
9.
10.

SOUNDS EASY DOESN'T IT?

But you know change sometimes isn't that easy

Remember all those failed New Year's resolutions? Promises to change that seem hard. Or maybe we forget, or find we can't be bothered, or talk ourselves out of things.

So, let's recognise something. It's hard to make changes. That's why we've asked you to pick activities to do that you know can be good for you.

But if you find you get stuck doing a particular activity, here's a helping hand to make a plan to do it that will work.

Turn over to make your plan.

Don't just sit there, make a plan!

Planner sheet

1. What am I going to do?

2. When am I going to do it?

3. What problems or difficulties could arise, and how can I overcome them?

Is my planned task -

Q. Useful for improving
   my well-being?

Yes   No
☐   ☐

Q. Specific, so that I will
   know when I have done it?

Yes   No
☐   ☐

Q. Realistic, practical
   and achievable?

Yes   No
☐   ☐

HOW DID IT GO?

Life's all about learning

If you make a plan and everything goes smoothly- that's great!

But you can also learn a lot from when things go wrong too. So, if there are problems with your plan - that's great too. It's great because you can play detective and learn.

So, if you got stuck, or something was difficult, ask yourself some questions. Was the problem something *internal* – inside you, or *external* – for example a problem caused by someone else, the weather, or unexpected circumstances?

Use whatever you discover to make your next plan even better.

You'll find a useful Review sheet to help you with this learning on the next two pages.

Try to get into a sequence of *Plan* (using the Planner sheet), *Do*, and *Review* (using the Review sheet) for whenever you are planning more difficult activities. That way you will keep moving forwards.

OK, how did it go?

Review Sheet

What did you plan to do? Write it here:

If yes:

1. What went well?

2. What didn't go so well?

3. What have you learned from what happened?

4. How are you going to apply what you have learned?

Did you try to do it?

Yes

No

If no: what stopped you?

Internal things (forgot, not enough time, put it off, didn't think I could do it, couldn't see the point etc.).

External things (other people, work or home issues etc.).

How could you have planned to tackle these things?

HANG ON!

What if it doesn't work?

Don't worry if you don't finish your plan. Just getting started will be cycle-busting, and help you to feel better.

If you find that you get stuck halfway through, just sit down and think about why -

- Are the steps too big or hard?
- Would it have been better if you had chosen some other activity?
- Do you need to do a bit of unblocking?

If so, just go back to the beginning of this chapter, make another plan and have a go at that.

There's no reason to beat yourself up - you're doing great! You're working on a plan!

Things to watch out for

Don't try and make every change possible all at once.

Be realistic – you're planning for success not a let-down. You know your own personality and how inpatient or ambitious you are. That's where it's important to be wise and plan just one main change a day to start with.

So, pick just a few things to get you started, and make a separate plan to do each using the Planner sheet. Then plan them in across the day and the week .

1. Leave some gaps for the unexpected things that crop up.

2. Include some time just for you.

3. Add in some more routines like a regular time to do the household jobs, or perhaps to go for a walk, meet friends or go to school.

4. Make sure your plan fits with your values/ideals of how you want to live.

But don't forget that some things are important to do even if they aren't much fun or seem difficult.

AT THE END OF EACH DAY

Use your Happy List to help you remember

Each evening, sit down and write down three things that you:

- Have enjoyed.

- Felt was a job well done.

- Or helped you feel close to someone else.

After a few days, you'll have a list of great things that you can look back on. It will help you remember how you're changing things.

Time to give yourself a pat on the back!

Go for it!

Introduction to Chapter 3

Have you ever looked through a Kaleidoscope? Everything seems beautiful and colourful. The red, green, yellow and blue shapes form in fantastic combinations and draw your attention.

How we think can be like that. We can choose to focus on the amazing, the good things, the people around us we like and who like us, the places we love and the hobbies and interests we enjoy.

But sometimes it can seem the opposite happens. We become focused on the difficulties - the challenges and the hard things in life. We may notice the things we haven't done more than the things we have done. We pick over our faults and weaknesses rather than celebrate the good things in our lives.

In this chapter you'll discover what Bad thoughts are and what they look like. Bad thoughts are thoughts that make us feel worse, in our feelings, bodies or relationships. Like celebrities they crave attention and always like to be in the spotlight. But maybe not everything they say is always true, helpful or accurate.

At times when we feel under pressure Bad thoughts pop into our minds more, and are harder to shift. They become a focus and start to make us feel even more stressed, down or emotional. Together they also cause us to react in ways that make things worse such as withdrawing from others, or doing things that can backfire on how we feel.

You'll learn some effective ways of relating differently to these upsetting bad thoughts. It will help you play detective, spot the bad thoughts and put them in their place.

Remember, you have control.

Chapter 3

LOOKING AT THINGS DIFFERENTLY

NOBODY LIKES ME

I ALWAYS MESS UP

EVERYONE THINKS
I'M A LOSER!

If I don't get this
sorted out, I won't cope

It's All My Fault

WHAT'S THE POINT?

Things never work
out for me

Sound familiar?

That's because loads of people think that way - but when you're already feeling pretty bad, thoughts like these make you feel even worse.

The fact is, bad thoughts **cause** bad feelings. It's not just the other way round. So one way to feel better is to do something about the bad thoughts.

This chapter will show you how.

Turn the page and we **guarantee** you'll feel better straight away.

GOOD MOVE!

You turned the page!

You didn't say "Oh, forget it!" and throw the book out - you turned the page and took a giant leap towards feeling better - by yourself.

Keep on turning and you'll find out how to keep on feeling better and better, with the

AMAZING BAD-THOUGHT-BUSTING PROGRAM

On the next two pages is a BAD THOUGHT SPOTTER.

Use it to check if you're having any of the usual thoughts that mess people up.

BAD THOUGHT SPOTTER

Bad thoughts are also known as unhelpful thinking styles.

Here are some examples to help you spot when your thinking isn't helping.

If you tick one or more boxes on the right, you've spotted a bad thought that you can fix with the **AMAZING BAD-THOUGHT-BUSTING PROGRAM**

Unhelpful thinking styles	Tick
Are you your own worst critic? Do you always seem to be beating yourself up about something?	
Do you focus on the bad stuff? As if you were looking at the world through darkened glasses?	
Do you have a gloomy view of the future? Expecting everything to turn out badly?	
Are you jumping to the worst conclusions? Thinking it's the end of the world.	
Do you assume that others see you badly? When you haven't checked whether it's true, it's called 'mind-reading'.	
Do you take responsibility for everything? Including things that aren't your fault?	
Are you always saying things like 'Should' and 'Got to'? Setting impossible standards for yourself?	

Turn the page to beat these bad thoughts

STEP 1

First, label the thought

When you notice one of your bad thoughts, don't get all screwed up, just mentally step back and stick a label on it.

"Oh, that's just one of those bad thoughts"

When you label a bad thought this way, **it** loses its power and **you** realise it's just part of being upset.

It's not the truth, it's just one of those bad thoughts.

You could even talk to it. Say: "You're caught! I'm not playing that game again!"

Turn over for **step 2**

NOW LEAVE IT ALONE

Mentally turn your back on the bad thought. Don't challenge it or try to argue with it, just let it be.

Bad thoughts love attention, so don't give them any.

Instead, think about what you're doing right now, or stuff that you're planning for the future, or things you've achieved lately

Step 3 next ...

STEP 3

STAND UP TO IT!

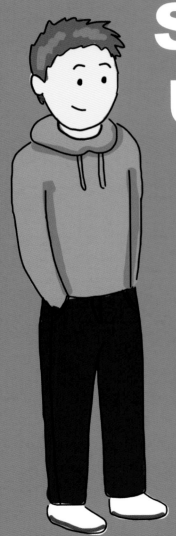

Don't be bossed around by bad thoughts

Bad thoughts can be intimidating. But although they sound strong, really they're weak underneath. And they tell lies.

They say you won't like doing something. They say you'll fail if you try. They tell you you're no good or you're scared or nobody likes you.

But this is just the bad thought, not the truth.

If the thought says "Don't!" then DO! If the thought says "Can't" say CAN! Right back at it.

Easy for us to say? You're right.

But just give it a try, one time. You'll find that you really can beat bad thoughts.

Turn over for the next step in the **Amazing Bad-Thought-Busting Program**

GIVE YOURSELF A BREAK!

Be a better friend to yourself, you deserve it

Bad thoughts are how we beat ourselves up when we're upset.

So if you're having trouble with a bad thought, think what the person who loves you most in the whole world would say to you, right now.

They'd disagree with the bad thought. They'd remind you that you're not a loser, or stupid, or bound to fail.

Trust these positive things and let them help get rid of the bad thoughts.

Turn over for step 5 - what to do about the **really** bad thoughts

HOW TO BEAT THE REALLY BAD ONES

Some bad thoughts are hard to beat.

They keep coming back and you wonder if you'll ever get the better of them.

Here are some questions you can ask that will help.

Look at the situation differently

First, imagine what it would be like if it was a friend, not you, who was having this bad thought. What advice would you give? Now give the same advice to yourself.

Put your thought or worry into perspective. Will it matter in six months? Will you even remember what the problem was? If it won't matter in six months, it's probably not that important now.

How would others deal with the problem? Think about someone who seems to handle problems well and work out what they would do, or how they would think in this situation.

Turn over to **recap**

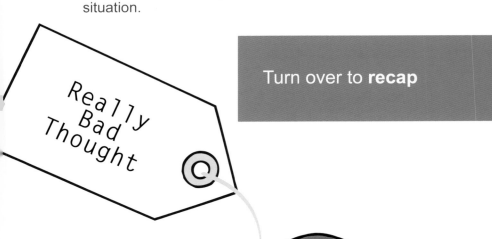

Really Bad Thought

Recap

SO:

The Amazing Bad-Thought-Busting Program

Bad thoughts mess you up and actually **cause** bad feelings. Beat bad thoughts and you'll feel better.

When you notice a bad thought:

1. Label it

Oh you're just one of those bad thoughts.

2. Leave it

A bad thought needs attention, so don't give it any.

3. Stand up to it

Bad thoughts are intimidating but weak underneath. You can beat them.

4. Give yourself a break

What would someone who really loved you say? Trust them and let them help you beat the bad thought.

5. Look at it differently

Give yourself the advice you'd give to a friend. Ask yourself if it will matter in six months.

So what are you waiting for? Let's try it out

The Amazing Bad-Thought-Busting Programme

1. Label it
Oh, you're just one of those bad thoughts.

2. Leave it
A bad thought needs attention, so don't give it any.

3. Stand up to it
Bad thoughts are intimidating but weak underneath.
You can beat them.

4. Give yourself a break

What would someone who really loved you say? Trust them and let them help you beat the bad thought.

5. Look at it differently

- Give yourself the advice you'd give a friend.
- Ask yourself if it will matter in six months.
- Pick someone you know and work out how they would handle the situation.
- Ask yourself if it matters so much.
- Are you basing this on how you feel rather than the facts?
- What would other people say?
- Are you looking at the whole picture?

GO DO IT!

Don't worry

If this seems hard at first.

It takes practice to beat bad thoughts.

But the Amazing Bad-Thought-Busting Program really works, so keep trying and within a few days, you'll have your bad thoughts on the run and be feeling better.

Remember the key thing is to plan to practice this approach.

Time to make a plan to practice it

Don't just sit there, make a plan!

Planner sheet

1. What am I going to do?

2. When am I going to do it?

3. What problems or difficulties could arise, and how can I overcome them?

Is my planned task -

Q. Useful for improving
my well-being?

Yes No

Q. Specific, so that I will
know when I have done it?

Yes No

Q. Realistic, practical
and achievable?

Yes No

Go for it!

MY PLAN
1 —
2 —
3 —

Introduction to Chapter 4

Can you think of someone you know who is really confident? It might be someone on television, or in a band? Or maybe a footballer or sports personality? What is it about them that makes them stand out as confident?

Is it how they stand? What they say or how they say it? Or is their confidence communicated through their clothes, hair or life style? Many young people look up to people like that, admire them and want to be more like them. The key in growing up isn't to try and act and be like someone else. Instead, it's to let the real you come out.

This chapter will help you discover the origins of confidence. The things that have been said to you that have encouraged you and given you confidence, or have drained confidence and left you with doubts. The good news is that we're learning new things all the time, and that can be true of confidence also. So, you just need to learn to trust and remind yourself of the many things that make you an OK person. You don't have to be a star to shine and be comfortable in yourself.

You will learn some positive things to remind yourself of whenever you feel small. You'll also get to practice some skills that will build your confidence to express yourself and present yourself well.

Finally, you'll also learn about the advantages and disadvantages of having high standards. High standards can push people to achieve good things. However high standards can also bring consequences. It can be stressful trying to live up to such standards, especially if you're struggling just now and feel under pressure. Instead, you'll learn that good enough is good enough.

You have the power to choose.

Chapter 4

BUILDING INNER CONFIDENCE

People don't like me

I'm not good looking

I just can't do it

I don't fit in

I'm not like everyone else

I'm boring

I mess everything up

I keep making mistakes

I DON'T LIKE ME

Who says you're not good enough?

You weren't born thinking 'I'm not good enough'. Someone or something made you feel that way, perhaps a long time ago.

Maybe your parents or carers didn't praise you or show that they cared enough. Maybe your classmates were cruel about your shape, size or abilities. Maybe you expect so much of yourself that 'failure' is bound to happen.

Whichever way the idea got into your head, the fact is it's there now, and it's been rattling around for so long that you believe it.

When you believe you're no good, you start to behave as if it's true - hiding away, not trying new things, keeping quiet about what you want, apologising all the time, not bothering to look after yourself. All of which means you don't live or enjoy your life as much as you could.

But you can change. This chapter contains an easy plan for replacing bad ideas (like 'I'm no good') with much more sensible ones (like 'I'm alright really').

Turn the page ...

WELL
DONE!

GOOD CHOICE

You chose to make a change

Keep doing that and your problems will soon be over.

How come? Well because it's so easy to believe ideas like "I'm useless" or "I'll never change." But these are just ideas that got into your head a while ago. If a different idea had got in there instead, like "I'm alright really," you'd feel a lot happier about yourself.

So what we're going to do in the next few pages is show you how to develop positive ideas about yourself, and put them into your head, where they should have been all along.

Then, when you have a choice of things to believe, you can pick the right one, like you did a minute ago.

Sounds simple, doesn't it? So what are you going to choose to do?

Keep reading ...

YOU'RE GETTING GOOD AT THIS!

So let's get some positive ideas going

If we told you the earth is flat, you wouldn't believe us, because you've been abroad and didn't drop off the edge. You have the evidence.

It's the same with ideas about yourself. It's hard to believe "I'm alright really" when you don't think you've got any evidence for it. So the first step in your plan is to spot some things you like about yourself and write them down.

Things you did well. Times you were helpful to others. Times you did something even when it was hard. Things you do that people really appreciate. Things you know a lot about. Things you can do easily or quickly. Times when you made a good contribution to a group activity.

Turn over and list some OK things about yourself

105

well done!

You turned to the OK THINGS list! It may take a while to come up with good stuff, because you've lost the habit of thinking you're OK. You are, though, so get writing!

Things I like about me

Remember, we're looking for things you did well, times you were helpful to others, people who like you and so on.

NOW LEARN YOUR LIST BY HEART

And say it to yourself whenever you feel small

You now have a list of reasons to believe you're OK, and every one is real and true, unlike those "I'm no good" ideas that sometimes come into your head.

Learn the list, and add more things to it as you think of them.

Keep repeating it so that it really sticks in your mind. Say it to yourself before going to sleep. Recite your list quietly when you have a moment to yourself.

I'm OK
I'm OK

After a while, it will help to replace some of the negative ideas that have been hanging around for so long.

Even better, you can also use your list in emergencies, whenever you get into a situation that makes you feel small.

Just read the list over and over again and it will start to change the other stuff. It's just like you did on the last few pages, choosing a more sensible option instead of the "I'm useless" one.

On the next page is a chart that could help you even more.

Turn over for more help ...

DON'T THINK THIS...

I can't do it

I'm not good looking

I'm boring

People don't like me

I'm not good at things

I mess everything up

THINK THIS

I can do it because I did (something from your list)

I look just fine

I'm interesting, I know about (something from your list)

Some people like me

I have strengths and weaknesses like everyone does

I'm good at (something from your list)

So you know how to change how you think.

What's next?

CHANGE WHAT YOU DO

How to build your confidence step by step

Everyone has an inside and an outside, and they're different.

You know those people who seem so confident? They're just like you inside, but they know a trick - walk confident, talk confident and you slowly become confident.

So what you need to do is be yourself and make some small, steady changes to let the real you shine.

To begin with, take a good look at how you present to others: Think about:

1. What you wear.

2. How you stand.

3. What you say, and how you say it.

You'll also need to become very observant ...

Now you get to make some changes ...

STEPS TO IMPROVING YOUR CONFIDENCE

How do other people do it?

Watch the way confident people stand. It's straight, isn't it? They often seem a bit taller than they really are.

Now pay attention to the way they hold themselves and move. There's no shuffling about, no slumping in chairs, no hiding in corners. And when they're speaking to you, they look you directly in the eye.

Now listen to the way they speak. They're pretty loud, aren't they? And they often speak quite slowly, not having to rush because they somehow know that everyone will keep on listening.

Your task is to slowly work towards this so people see the real you. Remember, most confident people aren't like that all the way through, they just know how to act confident on the outside.

After a while, you'll start to notice a real difference in how you present yourself and therefore start to feel better on the inside.

Turn over for more helpful hints

DON'T DO THIS

Mumble

Talk too quickly

Slump in your chair

Hunch over

Look away or look down

Shut down conversations

DO THIS

Try to speak a little louder and clearer

Slow down and pause while speaking

Sit up straight, shoulders back

Walk tall, lift your chin up

Make eye contact with others as much as possible and smile

Ask questions to get conversations going

AM I UP TO THIS?

Yes, you are!

It sounds like a lot to do, doesn't it?
To change your thinking and then start
practising ways to become a more confident
you.

But you only have to do these things a little
bit at first. Make that list of things you like
about yourself and just try reciting it once or
twice, when you feel small. Pick a confident
person and notice one of their mannerisms
to start with.

You won't become the life and soul of the
party overnight and you might not even
want to be that loud and bouncy anyway.

You're not here to become a big pop star or
a famous actor.

This way to a very important thing

GOOD
ENOUGH
IS GOOD
ENOUGH

Don't beat yourself up

In the real world, you don't have to get straight A's to be happy, successful and popular.

In fact the world's happiest people are those who are content with themselves as they are.

So whenever you're being hard on yourself for not doing something perfectly, not coming top of the class or finishing first in the race, say this to yourself -

There's no such thing as perfect. Just do what you can do

YOU'RE DOING FINE

Here's how to stay that way

1. Choose sensible ideas not bad ones

Fill in your list of things you like about you, learn it by heart and use it to change the negative ideas in your head.

Recite it to yourself before going to sleep. Use the list in situations that make you feel small and choose the "I'm OK" idea, not the "I'm useless" one.

2. Walk and talk with confidence

Remember, most confident people aren't like that all the way through, they just know how to act confident on the outside.

So do the same. Walk confident, talk confident, look confident and you'll be confident.

3. Remember, there is no such thing as perfect. Just do what you can do

Nobody's perfect, so don't beat yourself up because you can't reach an impossible goal.

So, here's what to do. Pick one small thing, then use the Planner sheet on pages 124-125 to give yourself the best start.

Once you're done, use the Review sheet on pages 126-127 to check your progress.

Go for it!

Don't just sit there, make a plan!

Planner sheet

1. What am I going to do?

2. When am I going to do it?

3. What problems or difficulties could arise, and how can I overcome them?

Is my planned task -

Q. Useful for improving
my well-being?

Yes **No**

Q. Specific, so that I will
know when I have done it?

Yes **No**

Q. Realistic, practical
and achievable?

Yes **No**

OK, how did it go?

Review Sheet

What did you plan to do? Write it here:

If yes:

1. What went well?

2. What didn't go so well?

3. What have you learned from what happened?

4. How are you going to apply what you have learned?

Did you try to do it?

Yes

No

If no: what stopped you?

Internal things (forgot, not enough time, put it off, didn't think I could do it, couldn't see the point etc.).

External things (other people, work or home issues etc.).

How could you have planned to tackle these things?

Download more from www.llttfyp.com

Introduction to Chapter 5

Most of us can tackle problems most of the time. But if there are too many challenges that we face all at once, or if the problems seem huge and overwhelming, then most of us can start to feel the pressure and begin to feel out of control.

It's so easy when we feel there's too much being demanded to feel daunted. We look at the amount of work, or the mountain of other demands we face and feel stuck, not knowing how to even start.

There's an added difficulty. At times when we feel stressed or down, we can find it difficult coming up with possible plans to sort out the problem. Even if we can come up with some solutions, if we feel stressed it's more likely we'll dismiss each possible response as not being likely to work.

The result is we feel trapped as if we are in a one way street and can't get out. All we focus on is the problem and our sense of powerlessness. So, what do we need to do? Just like that blind alley or a dead end you need to stop, look around and get clear where you are, then figure out how to plan your way out of there.

In this chapter you will learn an approach that you can use to tackle any problem. Yes, really, any problem. Whether you want to save or make some money, complete a homework project, tackle your brother or sister who is playing their music too loud when you're preparing for exams or even learn to play the guitar!

Remember, when it comes to problems, you'll learn a fresh and effective plan you can use.

Chapter 5
HOW TO FIX
ALMOST
EVERYTHING

IN 4 EASY STEPS

Finish a project

GET
ACTIVE

Gain some weight

SPEND
WISELY

Lose some weight

Get fitter

MAKE NEW
FRIENDS

Study for exams

Get out more

Yes, almost everything

It doesn't matter what you want to do, this easy 4-step plan will help you do it.

It works particularly well if you're feeling low. In fact it works even if you're so fed up you can only just be bothered reading this page.

The idea is to break your problem or target into tiny little chunks that, by themselves, are easy to do.

Then you work out how you're going to do each chunk, make a plan, and carry it out. It's called the Easy 4-Step Plan.

It's like getting up a climbing wall

HOW TO GET TO THE TOP OF AN ENORMOUS CLIMBING WALL

a. Break the climb into small steps
b. Take one step at a time

Problems are like climbing a wall

They look huge. Far too big to deal with.

But when you break them down into smaller bits, they're less intimidating and a lot easier to fix (or climb). That's why step 1 is 'break your problem into pieces'.

Let's say you feel you never see your friends outside of school. You could break the week into bits and make an effort to see them on Mondays, for example.

If you think you are spending too much time alone you could try watching TV with your family a couple of nights a week instead of sitting in your room. Why not phone your friends and have a conversation rather than texting? Or if you feel you're on social media or using apps too much, you could start by not checking it for an afternoon or a day.

Most problems can be chopped up like this, and you're much more likely to succeed when you do things bit by bit.

Turn over for Step 2

BRAINSTORM WAYS TO DO THE FIRST PIECE

Grab a piece of paper ...

And write down all the things you could do to work on the first bit of the problem.

The trick with brainstorming is to let your mind run free, and write everything down - the whacky things as well as the sensible ones.

To start seeing more of your friends, you could join an after school club that is held every Monday.

Spending too much time watching TV? You could get out one of those board games you like to play at holiday time as a family. Or ask a family member to play a sport with you. Or choose to chat about people's days as you eat in the evening.

Trying to cut down social media or apps? Leave your phone in another room. Or put it on silent for part of the day. Switch it off at a certain time in the evening ...

If you write everything down, there's bound to be a good idea in there somewhere.

STEP 3 next

CHOOSE AN IDEA AND MAKE A PLAN TO DO IT

Step by step

Look at your brainstorm ideas and pick one. Choose one that looks do-able and doesn't scare you too much.

Now take another piece of paper and write down, step by step, how to actually **do** it.

Make the steps as small as you like: Get up. Get dressed. Walk to front door. Open door ... and so on.

OR

To see friends after school more: text a friend, look at activities you could do together, sign up for an after school club, invite someone to your new favourite coffee shop ... like that.

OR

For using social media less: leave your phone in the other room, forget your phone on purpose one day when you go to school, set your phone and computer up to block some social media sites.

Make sure that the steps are small, straightforward and seem like things you could really do.

What if something gets in the way?

As soon as you've written your plan, think about what could stop it happening. Are there any unforeseen events that might trip you up? What about other people? Could someone be unhelpful at any stage?

When you've figured out what might block your progress, work out another mini-plan for getting round the obstacle.

This way, you'll be ready for whatever happens!

Final step coming up

CHECK THE PLAN AND PUT IT INTO ACTION

This is it! You've written down all the steps, now you need to check that they're do-able. Use this checklist:

Is it realistic?

You're not planning to run a marathon are you?

Are you aiming at just one thing?

Don't try and do more than one item on your list. You can always pick another when you've sorted the first one.

Is it slow?

There's no need to rush at things. Your plan can take as long as you like, as long as you stick to it, step by step.

Is it easy?

Make your steps small and easy and you'll be more likely to do them.

Are you ready to unblock it?

Have you thought about what could go wrong and how to deal with it?

Five ticks? ✓ ✓ ✓ ✓ ✓
Then go for it!

And that's how you do almost anything.

This Easy 4-Step Plan really works, whatever you want to do, so long as you follow it carefully, making all the steps really small and easy for yourself.

Still a bit doubtful?

THAT'S EASY FOR YOU TO SAY!

Don't worry, you can do it.

The Easy 4-Step Plan really works, even when you have a really tough problem to deal with.

Remember the climbing wall - you can get to the top step by step. All you have to do is keep on climbing!

And don't beat yourself up if things go wrong half way through. Just calmly go back to the plan and take those small, steady steps again.

But what about when your enthusiasm goes? When the novelty wears off and you can't remember why you went to all this trouble in the first place?

That's when you need the next two pages!

Easy 4-Step Plan

My problem

1. Break it into chunks

2. Brainstorm ways to do the first piece

3. Choose an idea and make a plan to do it

---

4. Check the plan and put it into action

Is it realistic? ☐

Are you aiming
at just one thing? ☐

Is it slow? ☐

Is it easy? ☐

Are you ready
to unblock it? ☐

NOW
DO IT

TRY OUT
YOUR
PLAN

Moving forward bit by bit

Now you have used the Easy 4-Step Plan to plan the first change, you need to do it. Sounds easy? But we all know sometimes we can get stuck or derailed. We may lose motivation, talk ourselves out of it, or maybe things change and we know the initial plan needs changing. Or we forget.

That's where making a clear plan to put what you've learned into action can help. The Planner sheet on the next two pages can really help. It helps provide a double check on your plan- and also forces you to be clear exactly what you are going to do and when you are going to do it.

Then, when you're done, review how you did using the Review sheet on pages 148-149.

Remember to work on your problem bit by bit using the Easy 4-Step and Planner sheets to plan each step one at a time (remember that climbing wall).

Don't just sit there, make a plan!

Planner sheet

1. What am I going to do?

2. When am I going to do it?

3. What problems or difficulties could arise, and how can I overcome them?

Is my planned task -

Q. Useful for improving
my well-being?

Yes **No**

Q. Specific, so that I will
know when I have done it?

Yes **No**

Q. Realistic, practical
and achievable?

Yes **No**

OK, how did it go?

Review Sheet

What did you plan to do?   Write it here:

If yes:

1. What went well?

2. What didn't go so well?

3. What have you learned from what happened?

4. How are you going to apply what you have learned?

Did you try to do it?

Yes ☐   **No** ☐

If no: what stopped you?

Internal things (forgot, not enough time, put it off, didn't think I could do it, couldn't see the point etc.).

External things (other people, work or home issues etc.).

How could you have planned to tackle these things?

WHAT TO DO WHEN THE GOING GETS TOUGH

Remind yourself why you're doing this

If you're having trouble keeping going, say, in the middle of your plan when things are getting difficult, try these ideas to remind yourself why you started in the first place.

- Write down the reasons you want to do this and put them where you can see them.

- Think about the position you'll be in in 2 or 3 years time if you give in now. Write that down and stick it where you can see it.

- Think about the advantages of succeeding - better health, better relationships, enjoying school more, having more friends, having more fun, having more money, doing better overall. Write those down and put them where you can see them.

- Tell as many people as possible what you're doing, so that they can help you (or remind you when you slip).

Ready for some real-life examples?

If you're not sure how to apply the Easy 4-Step Plan to your problem the next few pages will help.

They're full of real plans, showing how people like you have fixed different things and turned their lives around.

How the Easy 4-Step Plan works in real life

I want to make new friends

Step 1

How do you break 'making new friends' into little steps? Change it to 'make *one* new friend'. It's a lot easier to work at finding and connecting with one person than to try to transform yourself into the life and soul of the party.

So let's say your chosen step is 'Find and make one new friend'. You can always repeat the process when you've succeeded.

Step 2

Here's how your brainstorm might go:

- List the people you know already that you'd like to be a friend

- List the people who you haven't spoken to or hung out with for a while

- Stop eating alone in the cafeteria and sit with other people

- Ask people you know to introduce you to other people

- Join a club or society. If it involves sports or fitness, you could crack two problems at once!

Step 3

Let's choose idea 1 (List the people you know already that you'd like to be a friend) and make a plan.

- Make a list of the people who you met briefly and those who you added on Facebook, Instagram etc. or swapped numbers with but have never contacted.

- If you have no way of contacting them but you know their name, add them on Facebook etc.with a friendly message. Now take a look at those whose numbers you do have, and those who are already your friends on social media.

- Choose one person and text or call them up, or send them a message on Facebook etc. Invite them to study with you, go for coffee or go to a gig. If they are someone you know from school, ask them if you can borrow their book or ask them a question about a difficult piece of work.

Repeat this process with the next person on your list.

Step 4

Check the plan (see pages 138-139) and if you have 5 ticks, go for it.

And remember, if this plan doesn't work out, or it gets too much for you in the middle, don't beat yourself up, just go back to the brainstorm and pick another idea to try!

you can do it!

I need to study for exams

Step 1

Almost everyone is worried about exams and sometimes you can get like a deer in the headlights - there's so much to do, so many subjects to study that you just can't get started.

This is where the chunking idea is really handy - and really obvious. Don't try and study everything, just do one subject at a time. So your chunks could be:

History, Geography, English, Maths, Science ... and so on. What chunk to choose? Let's say History - that's **Step 1**.

Step 2

A brainstorm about ways to study History could come up with ideas like these:

- Make a list of the chapters you need to read and go through them one by one

- Make a timetable so that you cover everything by the exam

- Find a friend who's doing the same exam and work together

- Divide your week into study periods and don't go out or watch TV at those times.

- Decide on three days a week for study and text your friends to say your phone will be off on those days.

- Pitch a tent in the garden and do all your studying in there, away from the TV.

- Go to the library and get some books out about studying techniques.

Step 3

Let's say you choose idea 3 - find a friend and work together. This is what your plan could include.

- Call your friends in the same class, one by one, and outline your idea.

- Do a deal with the first one who agrees.

- Get together and decide on a day to start work

- Decide on a place to work

- Discuss the study methods you will use - testing each other?

- Have a plan for when motivation fades.

- Discuss and agree on a system of small rewards for good work. Maybe the cinema once a week.

Step 4

Check your plan for 5 ticks (pages 138-139) and put it into action.

And remember, you'll need motivation, especially when you've done the first couple of subjects and you're switching to maths, or something you don't like.

Here are some of the things you could stick on the wall of your study room to remind you why you're doing this:

- Better exam results mean a better career and more money

- Bad exam results mean little choice of what you do in life

- Bad exam results only mean you'll have to do it all again next year

- More people fail exams through not working

- You'll feel great when you've done each subject and can reward yourself

- A good performance in exams usually means a great summer holiday.

you can do it!

NOW IT'S YOUR TURN!

As the real life examples show, the Easy 4-Step Plan works really well. All you have to do is take it step by step and be steady and determined.

If one of the ready-made plans you've just seen fits the bill, please use it!

If you need to make one for yourself, get that piece of paper now and start breaking your problem into pieces you can tackle one step at a time!

Go for it!

Introduction to Chapter 6

We probably all would like to think we deal with life's challenges in effective and planned ways. Taking the long view and making the healthy choice. But also, if we're honest, that's not always the case. There may be decisions that we each make that make sense as a short term fix, but which come back to cause problems down the line.

There are many choices in life. Some of the most important choices are around when is there too much of a good thing. Think about ice-cream. A single cone is great. Maybe a double cone with the sprinkles on top? Or you could add a chocolate flake? But how many ice-creams can you have at once without feeling sick? Two? Four? What about 24?

There are other life examples like this where something can be healthy, normal and a good thing to do in moderation. So, if someone wants to ask the opinion of a trusted friend about some piece of work they have done, that can be really helpful – and provide useful and constructive feedback. But what if someone starts to feel anxious and doubts themselves and what they do. As a result they start to ask all their friends what they think. They doubt their own choice and keep changing things based on others opinions. Soon their confidence falls even more and they fall into a cycle of seeking reassurance again and again. To start with their friends are happy to comment, but that good will wears thin when the same question is asked for the 17th time that day.

There are lots of other life choices like this- where the key is to decide how to make sensible choices about what we do.
This chapter will help you discover what makes a choice helpful or unhelpful, and help you identify early signs that difficulties are occurring.

Above all, remember, you have choices to make as to how you choose to respond – helpfully or unhelpfully. Your choice.

Chapter 6

THE THINGS YOU DO THAT MESS YOU UP

AND HOW TO STOP DOING THEM

HIDING AWAY

Not eating

Binge drinking

EATING FOR COMFORT

COMPLAINING

Lashing out at people

Shoplifting

Self harming

TAKING DANGEROUS RISKS

Gossiping

Seeking reassurance all the time

If it makes me feel better, why should I stop?

"Just leave me alone" or "What I need now is chocolate!" We've all said it, and most of the time it's not a problem at all.

But when you're feeling down, the things that get you through can also become the things that mess you up.

One bar of chocolate becomes a comfort eating habit. One scratch becomes a cycle of risky self-harm. One question "Are you still my friend?" becomes a constant need for reassurance.

And instead of getting better, you get worse.

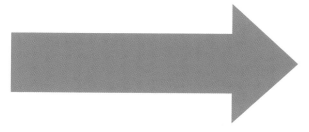

But this doesn't need to happen! Turn the page and you'll be taking the first step towards getting in control of the things you do.

YOU'RE ON YOUR WAY!

The first step is the most important

And you just took it. You made the decision to stop letting unhelpful behaviours mess up your life.

Now, we're going to help you work out what you're doing too much of, and then show you a simple 4-step way to stop or cut down.

How do you know when something is messing you up?

Turn over

IT'S NOT WHAT YOU DO, IT'S HOW MUCH YOU DO IT

We're not trying to be the fun police. There's nothing wrong with chocolate, spending some time alone or a bit of retail therapy.

But when you're feeling low, you can start to lean on these things, using them to help get you through a bad time.

Other, not so obvious behaviours can also be 'props'. Like lashing out at other people - physically or just by shouting. Cutting yourself. Hiding away from the world.

Trouble is, too much of this kind of stuff makes you worse, not better. You get into a kind of vicious cycle, doing something that seems to help for a bit, but finding that it actually makes life worse in the long run.

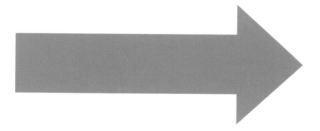

Turn the page and check whether you're doing too much of something.

Eating for comfort	Eating chocolate, etc. occasionally	Eating a little when you feel upset
Complaining	You say clearly what you feel and need	You moan a lot that "It's not fair"
Lashing out at people	You're sometimes rude when frustrated	You begin to blurt out hurtful things without even thinking
Gossiping	You tell others good news about your friends	You discuss good news told in confidence
Shoplifting	Your friends say they shoplift and you don't tell them it's wrong	You are with friends when they steal and don't say anything
Hiding away	You tend to be quiet in conversations	You avoid spending time with people

Eating a lot when you feel upset	Binge eating food when you're upset	Bingeing and making yourself sick when you're upset
You get really upset if you don't get your own way	You get really worked up and upset others too	You are so upset you don't get on with things and fall out with everyone
You often hurt people you don't like	You lash out at people you love when you feel frustrated	You get into fights often - hurting people and being injured yourself
You love to discuss people's private secrets	You get a reputation as someone who can't be trusted	No one trusts you and you feel lonely
You steal something small and say "it's no big deal"	You steal bigger and bigger things more and more often	Your shoplifting continues and you start to steal in other ways too
You go out of your way to cross the road to avoid chats with people you know	You lose confidence and find it hard even knowing where to start a conversation	You stay in all the time feeling anxious, panicky and depressed

Want to stop or cut down? **Turn over!**

OK. SO YOU
NEED TO
WORK ON
SOMETHING

Here's how ...

First, don't beat yourself up. Most people get into a cycle of doing unhelpful things when they're feeling down.

The fact that you're reading this means you're on the way to fixing it.

All you have to do is choose one problem behaviour to work on.

First choose a problem

The Things You Do That Mess You Up Checklist

Are you:

Eating for comfort or not eating enough	Where food becomes a marker of how you feel inside	Tick ☐
Taking recreational drugs	You can feel good without them	Tick ☐
Spending too much	It's called 'retail therapy'	Tick ☐
Taking dangerous risks	You can cause yourself real damage	Tick ☐
Self-harm	It doesn't help	Tick ☐
Being clingy	It pushes people away	Tick ☐
Lashing out at people	It can leave you feeling so alone	Tick ☐
Bullying	It's not really strong	Tick ☐
Shoplifting	It's not too exciting getting a criminal record	Tick ☐
Hiding away	Spirals down so you lose more and more confidence	Tick ☐

Are you:

Being impulsive about important things	e.g. Resigning a job without really thinking it through	
Setting yourself up to fail/ be rejected	Doing things that deliberately backfire	
Becoming a TV / Internet addict	It's no substitute for real relationships	
Wanting others to sort out every problem	It takes away your confidence	
Doing, doing, doing	You have no time for your own needs	
Drinking too much coffee/ cola to perk yourself up	It messes up your sleep	
Sleeping in the whole day	You won't sleep well at night	
Putting things off	Frustrating for you & others	
Worrying all the time	Things go round & round but problems don't get sorted out	

Other: please write any other things you do that mess you up

This way to something good

NOW CHOOSE SOMETHING TO DO THAT HELPS

Choose a sensible response instead

Just one tiny change to what you do and how you react can make all the difference.

Like what?

Well, how about planning and preparing for a good night's sleep. Or why not try doing something that makes you feel better, such as a hobby, having a relaxing bath, or listening to music? Pick something that you think you might feel motivated to do, and of course something that you think you could keep working at.

There are many helpful things that you could do. Choose one or more that you might do instead of the things you do that mess you up.

Helpful things checklist ahead!

Then follow our Easy 4-Step Plan to get control.

The Things You Do That Help Checklist

Are you:

Eating regularly and healthily	Taking time to enjoy the food	Tick ☐
Giving yourself time to sleep	It's a good start to any day	Tick ☐
Keeping up with routine things	Tidying your room, doing homework	Tick ☐
Doing things with other people	Spending time with family and friends or calling them on the phone	Tick ☐
Doing things that cheer you up	e.g. Hobbies, listening to music, having a nice bath	Tick ☐
Sharing problems with trusted friends and family	It can really help	Tick ☐
Finding out more about how you feel	For example: attending a voluntary sector self-help group	Tick ☐
Letting upsetting thoughts just be	Stop, think and reflect on things rather than just assuming upsetting thoughts are true	Tick ☐

176

Are you:

Facing your fears	Using slow steady steps	Tick ☐
Doing exercise / going for walks / swimming etc.	It can make you feel better	Tick ☐
Using your sense of humour to cope	Laughter always helps	Tick ☐
Planning time for you as well as for others	Not giving all the time	Tick ☐
Regularly taking the medicine prescribed by your physician	It can be part of the recovery process	Tick ☐
Relaxing	CDs, DVDs, baths, whatever works for you	Tick ☐
Using people around you	Your practitioner, family or friends - get them all on the job	Tick ☐
Doing the essentials	Don't let homework build up	Tick ☐

Q: Am I doing other things that help? Write in what you are doing if this applies to you

Easy 4-Step Plan this way

Break the problem into pieces

It's hard to stop doing something all at once, especially if you've been doing it for ages, so break it into easy chunks.

Let's say you feel you never see your friends outside of school. You could break the week into bits and make an effort to see them on Mondays, for example.

If you think you are spending too much time alone you could try watching TV with your family a couple of nights a week instead of sitting in your room. Why not phone your friends and have a conversation rather than texting? Or if you feel you're on social media or using apps too much, you could start by not checking it for an afternoon or a day.

Most problems can be chopped up like this, and you're much more likely to succeed when you do things bit by bit.

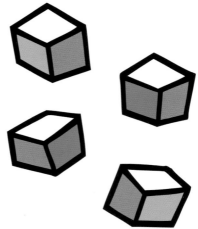

Brainstorm ways to do the first piece

Grab a piece of paper and write down all the things you could do to work on the first bit of the problem.

To start seeing more of your friends, you could join an after school club that is held every Monday.

Spending too much time watching TV? You could get out one of those board games you like to play at holiday time as a family. Or ask a family member to play a sport with you. Or choose to chat about people's days as you eat in the evening.

Trying to cut down social media or apps? Leave your phone in another room. Or put it on silent for part of the day. Switch it off at a certain time in the evening.

The trick with brainstorming is to let your mind go, and write everything down - the weird things as well as the sensible ones.

Go to the cinema

Join a club

Buy a book

Turn over for steps 3 and 4

Choose an idea and make a plan to do it

Look at your brainstorm ideas and pick one that looks do-able.

Now take another piece of paper and write down, step by step, how to actually **do** it.

Make the steps as small as you like: Get up. Get dressed. Walk to front door. Open door ... and so on.

OR

To see friends after school more: text a friend, look at activities you could do together, sign up for an after school club, invite someone to your new favourite coffee shop ... like that.

OR

For using social media less: leave your phone in the other room, forget your phone on purpose one day when you go to school, set your phone and computer up to block some social media sites.

Make sure that the steps are small, straightforward and seem like things you could really do.

What if something gets in the way?

As soon as you've written your plan, think about what could stop it happening. Is there anything that might trip you up? Could someone else be unhelpful at any stage?

When you know what could block your progress, make a mini-plan for getting round the block.

This way, you'll be ready for whatever happens!

Check the plan and put it into action

This is it! You've written down all the steps, now you need to check that they're do-able. Use this checklist:

Is it realistic?
You're not planning to run a marathon are you?

☐

Are you aiming at just one thing?
Don't try and do more than one item on your list. You can always pick another when you've sorted out the first one.

☐

Is it slow?
There's no need to rush at things. Your plan can take as long as you like, so long as you stick to it, step by step.

☐

Is it easy?
Make your steps small and easy and you'll be more likely to do them.

☐

Are you ready to unblock it?
Have you thought about what could go wrong and how to deal with it?

☐

Five ticks? ✓✓✓✓✓
Then go for it!

NOW
IT'S
YOUR
TURN!

Just take it step by step

Even a problem that seems huge can be tackled with the Easy 4-Step Plan. The secret is breaking everything down into small, manageable pieces.

When you're making your plan, be sure that the steps are small and do-able.

When you're doing your plan, take it step by step and if things get scary in the middle, give yourself a rest or a breather.

Then get back on track, taking one small step at a time until you've put your plan into action.

Be steady and determined, use the Easy 4-Step Plan and you **will** be able to stop doing the things that mess you up!

Use the Planner sheet on the next two pages to help you plan these changes.

Go for it!

Don't just sit there, make a plan!

1. What am I going to do?

2. When am I going to do it?

3. What problems or difficulties could arise, and how can I overcome them?

Is my planned task -

Q. Useful for improving
my well-being?

Yes   **No**

Q. Specific, so that I will
know when I have done it?

Yes   **No**

Q. Realistic, practical
and achievable?

Yes   **No**

Introduction to Chapter 7

Do you always stay calm? Relaxed when your baby sister pours milk over your art project? Happy when someone says something bad about you to others? Unless you're a Saint (and we think even Saints lose their tempers sometimes!) there will probably be things every day or every week that make us feel annoyed.

Anger can sometimes be appropriate. If something unjust happens it's entirely healthy and normal to get annoyed – things like poverty, injustice, inequality ... the list goes on of things we should all be angry about. However whether that anger is productive and helpful is also about the choices we make in how we respond.

How we choose to respond when we feel annoyed really matters. Do we lose control and throw a tantrum? Do we shout, or swear or lash out? When we lose control like that we might feel powerful for a time- but in the longer term we can end up becoming isolated. People move away and give us a wide berth, they may be wary of us, and we can feel bad because we lost it rather than responding maturely.

So, how can we slow things down when we start to get angry so we respond in better ways? Mature ways that solve problems rather than adding to them? Again, it involves choices – choices to respond differently. This chapter tells you how to do this and gain control so your anger works for you rather than against you.

Chapter 7

1, 2, 3 BREATHE

TAKING CHARGE OF ANGER AND IRRITABILITY

Don't laugh at me

Turn that music down

GOT A PROBLEM WITH THAT?

She just pushes my buttons

Don't answer me back

YOU MAKE ME DO THIS!

You never listen

Are you looking at me?

He was asking for it

DON'T TALK TO ME LIKE THAT

He really winds me up

Excuses, excuses

What 'reason' do you use when you lose your cool?

Did someone else say something, do something or forget to do something? Was it a teacher, parent, guardian or sports coach who pushed your buttons?

Anger can have a helpful role. It can get you motivated to respond and change things. But if it gets out of control, it can get you into trouble, into hospital, out of relationships and out of school.

Lose your temper all the time and you'll probably lose everything, eventually.

And anyway, temper tantrums are for kids, not young adults.

They're what you do when you lose it. When all you can think of is throwing your toys out of the pram. When you don't know the difference between being strong and being aggressive.

Know what we think?

IT'S WEAK TO STAY AND ARGUE

Doesn't sound right, does it?

A lot of people say that standing your ground is strong, that you should look up to people who don't take any nonsense.

But think about it. What happens when you lose your temper? Things get out of control and you get into trouble. People stay away from you. You end up on your own.

What's so strong about that?

Wouldn't it be better **not** to shout and lash out? Wouldn't it be better to be admired for being calm and in control?

This chapter can help you do that, but you'll have to be strong. A lot stronger than your angry self.

Strong stuff next

IT'S STRONG TO KEEP YOUR COOL

Get a different plan

Strong, calm, controlled people choose to avoid aggravation in the first place, or they choose to react differently when they feel their blood start to boil.

It takes real strength to do this. It's much easier to lose it, shout or swear, stamp your feet or throw a punch.

But this chapter will help you take the tougher option. When you use the 3-step plan that comes later, you'll really get to know your own temper and how to keep it under control.

You'll become calmer, quieter, more powerful. And the people who count will know that you're a much stronger person than you used to be.

YOU GOT A PROBLEM WITH THAT?

It's not strong to lose it

If you still think losing control of yourself isn't stupid, think about this:

Imagine you've passed your driving test. You're driving a car quite fast and you come to a tight bend with a slippery surface. You're going to need all your skill to stay on the road, so you take a deep breath, remember everything you've learned about driving, grip the wheel and control the car until the danger is past.

What would happen if you lost it, instead? If you let a red mist come down and got angry at the bend because it was too tight? You'd skid, wouldn't you? You, the car and your passengers would end up in the ditch, in the hospital or in the graveyard.

In your life, you're always in that car. Your aim is to finish your journey in one piece. That slippery bend is just something that 'pushes your buttons'.

Use your skill to stay in control and you stay alive. Lose your temper and you don't.

Lost it!

Now ask what's in it for you

WHAT'S IN IT FOR ME?

Big respect

The self-respect you earn when you stay in control and use your skill and strength to handle a tough situation.

The respect of your friends and family who look at you in a new way and start to realise that you're stronger than they thought.

The respect of strangers who, when you speak calmly or walk away from angry situations, know that you helped to make things better, not worse.

There's not much that's more important than respect. If you agree, and think you're strong enough to try our 3-step plan, turn the page and …

Let's get started!

IT'S EASY TO BE STRONG

As easy as ...

 Know your buttons. Think about what makes you angry. The people or places that always seem to get you going. When you know your buttons, you can keep them from being pressed.

 Know your early warning system. You feel different just before you snap. With some people it's heavy breathing. Others feel the blood pounding in their ears. Learn to spot these signs so you can move to step 3 before they turn into trouble.

 Know where the escape hatches are. You just decide to react differently this time. Some people pause and count to 10, or decide to walk away. Others have phrases that they say, that defuse a situation. When you have a few of these up your sleeve, you'll be able to stay in control whatever happens.

Breathe!

As soon as you've escaped, give yourself respect. You're strong. You're in control. You've steered the car round that slippery corner without losing it. You've been strong enough to keep your temper.

So let's do it!

KNOW YOUR BUTTONS

What always gets you going?

Something your parent or guardian always says? Or your brother or sister? What about your friends? Other kids or teachers at school?

These are all buttons. You need to think about them so that you know exactly which ones apply to you. Then you need to write them down on the next 2 pages.

Why? Because when you know your buttons, you can keep them from being pressed. Go to different places. Spend time with different friends. Ignore other people's comments. Get control of the car, steer round the corner and forget about what other drivers are doing.

Being told off

Being ignored

Feeling left out

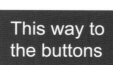

This way to the buttons

My buttons

Write down the things make you lose your temper or get irritable.

What gets me going?

What gets me going?

Step 2 next

KNOW YOUR EARLY WARNING SYSTEM

Feeling tense?

Think about the last time you lost your temper. How did you feel just beforehand? Can you remember what happened, physically or mentally?

You may have started breathing heavily, clenched your fists, stood up suddenly, folded your arms, drummed on the table with your fingers. Some people really do see a red mist in front of their eyes.

Or maybe your early warnings are in your mind. You start to feel critical of someone else. You don't think much of their appearance, their voice, their clothes, their opinions. Maybe you feel ignored or think people are looking down on you.

All these signs are really useful, because they warn you that you're getting near to losing it. They're like a road sign that says 'Slippery corner ahead'.

Think about the signs that apply to you and write down as many as you can on the next two pages.

List this way

My early warning system

Write down all the things you think and feel, just before you lose it.

> Feeling hot or breathing hard for example

What to do when you
start to feel this way

USE THE ESCAPE HATCH

This is when you react differently

Here's when you count to 10, or change the subject, or walk away, or sit down, relax your shoulders and breathe deeply.

Some people 'switch on' some music in their head when they get one of their early warning signs.

Others have a few words that they whisper to take the heat out of the situation ('watch the road ahead' are good ones).

You need to have a choice of escape hatches and be ready to use one whenever you get an early warning sign.

You can invent your own, of course, that fit with the buttons you wrote down earlier. Or you can turn the page and see some of the Escape Hatches that other people use. They won't mind you borrowing them.

More ideas this way

MORE ESCAPE HATCHES

Smile

When your face or fists are tensing up, make yourself smile and feel the aggravation go away. Don't just bare your teeth, give out a proper big smile that lights up your face. Others will notice, and things will calm down.

Say "You might be right about that"

This works best when you really disagree with someone. Instead of arguing and getting angry, just say "You might be right about that". You don't have to mean it, it's an escape hatch. Often, the other person will be so surprised that all the tension will drain away.

Sit down

When we're about to burst,
we need to be standing, so we
can fight, or run, or seem bigger
than we are. It's a lot harder to get into
trouble when you're sitting down though, so
when you get an early warning, stay in your
seat, or go find one.

Hum

We're serious. What's your favourite song?
Get into the habit of humming it to yourself
when you get an early warning. Use it to
change you focus. It works even better with
slow, calming tunes.

And finally

1 2 3 Breathe!

BREATHE

Relax your shoulders and breathe slowly

Often, your shoulders are up around your ears when tension builds. If you notice this in time and make a point of relaxing and letting them drop, you'll calm yourself and others too. Breathe slowly and think about slippery corners while you do it.

When you breathe, close your mouth - it's hard to over breathe though your nose.

And as you breathe - reconnect with your body and surroundings. Use it to centre yourself - to step back and notice your reactions. Stop, think and reflect. Use the breaths to focus and change how you react.

Feels great doesn't it?

1 2 3 Breathe!

SO NEXT TIME...

Follow the plan

 Know your buttons. Get to know the buttons on your list. When you know them, you can keep them from being pressed.

 Know your early warning system. Learn your danger signs and look out for them so that you can move to step 3 before they turn into trouble.

 Know where the escape hatches are. React differently. Count to 10, walk away, say the phrase, hum the tune. Whatever your chosen escapes are, use one as soon as you get an early warning sign.

Breathe!

Now give yourself credit.

You're in control - you've responded well. You've steered the car round that slippery corner without losing it. You've handled things well.

Now, time to make a plan. Pick one small thing to practice or change. Then use the Planner sheet on the next two pages to give yourself the best start.

Once you're done, use the Review sheet on pages 218-219 to check your progress.

Go for it!

Don't just sit there, make a plan!

Planner sheet

1. What am I going to do?

2. When am I going to do it?

3. What problems or difficulties could arise, and how can I overcome them?

Is my planned task -

Q. Useful for improving
my well-being?

Yes **No**

Q. Specific, so that I will
know when I have done it?

Yes **No**

Q. Realistic, practical
and achievable?

Yes **No**

OK, how did it go?

Review Sheet

What did you plan to do? Write it here:

If yes:

1. What went well?

2. What didn't go so well?

3. What have you learned from what happened?

4. How are you going to apply what you have learned?

Did you try to do it?

Yes

No

If no: what stopped you?

Internal things (forgot, not enough time, put it off, didn't think I could do it, couldn't see the point etc.).

External things (other people, work or home issues etc.).

How could you have planned to tackle these things?

Introduction to Chapter 8

We all want to feel happier don't we? To enjoy things, to feel and live in healthy ways, and to appreciate the good things around us. But sometimes it can seem so hard. This chapter makes a remarkable claim. That there are some things that we can all choose to do which can help start to make us feel happier straight away. Each of the things are small achievable actions that can have powerful impacts on how we feel.

But setting up new habits can feel hard. Think back to the start of the year and all the New Year Resolutions that each of us can make- and often fail to keep. What causes a failed resolution? Being unrealistic? Maybe trying to do it all by yourself? Maybe beating yourself up mentally if you have a setback? There's so many things that can make change hard. That's why this chapter- and each of the other the chapter's ends with the idea of making a plan. Having a Plan gives you direction. It helps you plan what you'll do and when you'll do it. That pattern of *Plan, Do* and *Review* (using the Planner and Review sheets) is a pattern you can use to take forward the lessons of this chapter, this book and the linked course.

So, as you come to this final topic, remember you have choices and control going forward in your life. Use the Planner and Review sheets to help you make effective plans, so you move forward learning all the time. That way, you really will move towards living life to the full.

Chapter 8
10 THINGS YOU CAN DO TO FEEL HAPPIER STRAIGHT AWAY

Seriously!

No Pills

No Booze

No Drugs

No Diets

No Supplements

No Preaching

No Pain

You can start feeling better about 10 minutes from now

Like loads of people, you're not feeling great at the moment.

Your system's a bit sluggish. You're miserable some of the time. You think your life could be better all round, but nothing seems to cheer you up these days.

So here's the good news: you can start to feel better in a few minutes from now. All you have to do is finish reading this chapter and then make some small, easy changes to what you do each day.

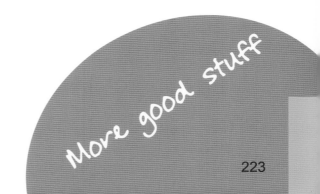

More good stuff

DON'T PANIC!

No broccoli is involved

You *will* have to get off the couch and walk about a bit. You'll also have to eat more healthily but you won't have to wear Lycra shorts and we promise not to turn you into a vegetarian.

The thing is this: there are things you can do and things you can eat that *make you feel happier straight away.*

Amazingly, some foods can help you get going to face the day. Some activities give your mood a major boost.

When you combine the two - eating healthily *and* doing certain things - those fed up feelings can disappear (along with spots sometimes).

And it's easy. You just make ten small changes to your daily routine.

Are you ready?

10
SMALL,
EASY
CHANGES

You need a clear head when you're changing your life

1. Get Outside More

2. Eat Good Things

3. Put on Your WOW Glasses

4. Call a Friend

5. Get Creative

6. Slow it Down

7. Make A Note of This

8. Take One Away

9. Do Something for Someone Else

10. The Happy List

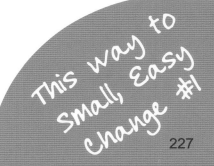

This way to Small, Easy change #1

GET OUTSIDE MORE

Enjoy the fresh air and exercise

Exercise is good for you. So good that when you do it, your body says 'thanks' by sending happy chemicals to your brain.

Go for a run, or enjoy a hike. Try an aerobics class, or kickboxing, or try a dance class. Go dancing whenever you can. Take a dog for a walk. If you don't have one then try borrowing one from a friend or neighbour- ideally an elderly neighbour who has difficulty walking. Remember to tell people where you are going and avoid walking after dark on your own.

Climbing stairs is one of the best ways there is to get fitter and get that happy stuff into your head. In fact climbing stairs each day for a year is the same as climbing a large mountain. Great view isn't it!

while you're out enjoying the fresh air, here's what to go and buy ...

EAT
GOOD
THINGS

Are you fed up with hearing about 5 a day?

Even if you like fruit and vegetables, it's hard to have five portions a day.

Trouble is, you really do need that much fibre. Without it, your system clogs up and you get all sad and sluggish.

So here's a cheat—drink smoothies.

Other things help too like porridge and muesli. They give you lasting energy and keep you regular.

You can also snack on fruit like bananas and strawberries, enjoying the taste, smell and textures.

Ready? Walk briskly to the store, buy the fruit, vegetables and granola you like.

Walk briskly home, mix and mash and have your first of five glasses, feel smug.

Got diabetes or watching your weight? Then choose low sugar fruits like berries, cherries, apples, grapefruit, pears, apricots, strawberries, and plums.

Small Easy change #3 next

PUT ON YOUR 'WOW' GLASSES

The world is amazing when you really look at it

When was the last time you went outside and really noticed what's there? The wind, the warmth, the cold, the rain, the trees, the flowers, the shops and the sky. When you stop and think, the world is full of stuff that makes you go 'Wow!'

People who recover from really bad times often say they appreciate things they used to take for granted. So put on your special glasses and see the world for the amazing place it is.

Even better do it with a friend. Go for walks together, talk about good times, and you'll soon get those happy feelings going through your brain.

TEST

IT

OUT

Use this page to rate your mood before and after your WOW walk.
Use it to discover the effect of your WOW walk on you.

Rate your mood
(Before your walk)

Happiness		Tick
Tension or anxiety		Tick
Closeness to others		Tick

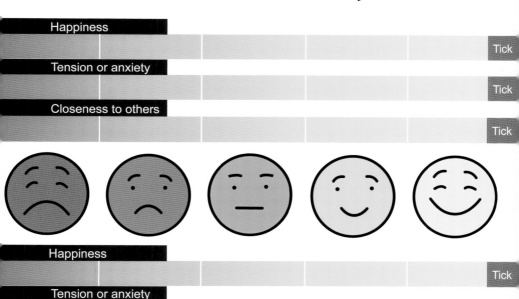

Happiness		Tick
Tension or anxiety		Tick
Closeness to others		Tick

Rate your mood
(After your walk)

CALL A FRIEND

It's good to talk

Connecting with others that you care about can make you feel good.

It's easy if you feel tired, or stressed, or fed up to go to your room and hide away. But that just worsens the problem. You feel isolated and have less things to talk about when you do meet up with others.

So, reach out. Pick up the phone, make a call, send a text or an email. Or post an update on social media that's fun and will get others commenting.

GET
CREATIVE

Act like a kid again

It's great to discover the excitement of creating something new that you've thought of and done by yourself.

What are you good at, - what do you enjoy?

Drawing, painting, gardening, taking photographs, writing a blog post, keeping a journal, playing or writing music, writing a poem or a rap, creating a mural in your bedroom, or even building something like a treehouse or a skateboard or a go-kart.

There's no better feeling than to see the end result.

SLOW
IT
DOWN

Just be ...

Try to focus on just one task at a time. So, don't watch television and go on social media at the same time. Put your phone away in your bag or pocket when you are speaking to someone.

- Breathe: drop your shoulders and focus on the breath

- Choose to sometimes read a book rather than using a phone or computer

- Take a long, hot bath

- Take the opportunity to talk and reconnect with people around you. You might find they are feeling the same way and have even more hints and tips you can use too

Oh, and while doing it ...

you could try the next idea

Don't suffer in silence

Music cheers you up. Obvious? So why are you sitting there in silence? Silence is just a space for you to think about your worries.

Put some of your favourite music on. Do it now. Play music while you're exercising and getting out of breath and it'll send even more happy stuff to your brain.

Play music while you're walking briskly to the shops. Play music while you're sitting around. Create a playlist for when you need a lift.

But don't play sad stuff, angry stuff, or songs that remind you of unhappy times. Keep it upbeat and you'll get an instant lift.

TAKE
ONE
AWAY

This one saves money too

Eating too much fast food or take away food is a great way to get really down.

Did you see that experiment where a man ate nothing but fast food? He felt depressed and really unhealthy within a couple of weeks.

So here's what you do: cut out one portion of fast food a week. Just one. Replace it with something you make yourself (easy things like pasta or rice are fine).

It won't change your life all at once, but put together the extra outdoor activity and healthier eating you're doing and within a few weeks you'll start to feel fitter and happier. And a bit better off.

DO SOMETHING FOR SOMEONE ELSE

It's not what you do, it's who you do it for

Do a small kindness for someone else, every day, and you'll feel even better than they do. What's more, you'll feel good straight away.

It doesn't have to be a big thing like sometimes helping at a soup kitchen or drop-in centre (although those would be great, of course).

You can just as easily get a lift in your mood by helping someone with their work, writing a letter of thanks for being your friend, cooking a meal or spending time with a person who needs the company.

Go on, sit down now and plan one or two helpful things you're going to do for other people this week. They'll feel good, but you'll feel even better!

Final idea coming up next

THE HAPPY LIST

Remember the good things

When you're down it's easy to forget the good times - times you've succeeded in something, things that make you smile and times you did something to help someone else.

So remember them. Each evening, sit down and write down three things that you:

- have enjoyed

- felt was a job well done

- or helped you feel close to someone else

After a few days, you'll have a list of great things that you can look back on, and this will help you feel a lot better.

What you think about affects how you feel. Focus on the good things and you'll be happier for it!

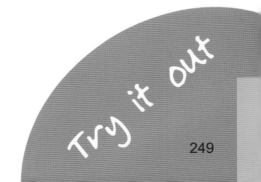

Try it out

MY
GOOD
TIMES

Write down all the things you've enjoyed, felt was a job well done, or has helped you feel close to someone else.

How much did it fit with your values/ideals of how you want to live your life? Is there anything to be thankful for?

WHAT ARE YOU WAITING FOR?

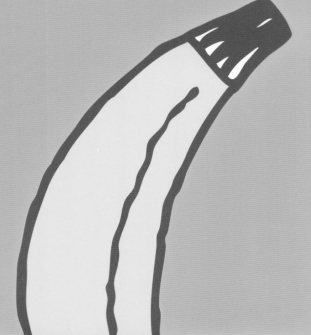

Go and get that banana

At the beginning of this chapter, we promised you could start feeling better in ten minutes. It's time, so here's what you do:

Pick one small thing then use the Planner sheet on the next two pages to give yourself the best start.

If it's daylight, go out, walk briskly to the shops and buy a couple of bananas. Walk quickly home and eat one or two.

If it's night and the shops are closed, walk up and down your stairs or jog on the spot for ten minutes, or long enough to get your heart pumping.

Whichever you do, you'll know you're making changes that make a difference.

Once you're done, use the Review sheet on pages 256-257 to check your progress.

Go make a plan

Don't just sit there, make a plan!

Planner sheet

1. What am I going to do?

2. When am I going to do it?

3. What problems or difficulties could arise, and how can I overcome them?

Is my planned task -

Q. Useful for improving
my well-being?

Yes	No
☐	☐

Q. Specific, so that I will
know when I have done it?

Yes	No
☐	☐

Q. Realistic, practical
and achievable?

Yes	No
☐	☐

OK, how did it go?

Review Sheet

What did you plan to do? Write it here:

If yes:

1. What went well?

2. What didn't go so well?

3. What have you learned from what happened?

4. How are you going to apply what you have learned?

Did you try to do it?

Yes **No**

If no: what stopped you?

Internal things (forgot, not enough time, put it off, didn't think I could do it, couldn't see the point etc.).

External things (other people, work or home issues etc.).

How could you have planned to tackle these things?

WHERE TO GET EVEN MORE ADVICE AND SUPPORT
(but no broccoli)

For more tips on feeling better, go to www.llttfyp.com. It's free, and it's packed with ways to lift your mood and start having a healthier life.

And don't worry, last time we looked, very few vegetables were mentioned.

Go for it!

LLTTF and the Bad Thought bug image are registered trademarks of Five Areas Resources Ltd.

Acknowledgements: We wish to thank Realspeak for their help with design and content, the Blue Wave Youth Team, CMHA and Mrs Ann McCreath for helping adapt this course for use with young people, Philip Munro and Grace Mayer for the illustrations and Tara Surr for typesetting.